Fact Finders®

AMERICAN INDIAN LIFE

The Cherokee
The Past and Present of a Proud Nation

by Danielle Smith-Llera

Consultant: Brett Barker, PhD
Associate Professor of History
University of Wisconsin-Marathon County

CAPSTONE PRESS
a capstone imprint

Fact Finders Books are published by Capstone Press,
1710 Roe Crest Drive, North Mankato, Minnesota 56003
www.capstonepub.com

Library of Congress Cataloging-in-Publication Data
Smith-Llera, Danielle, 1971–
The Cherokee : the past and present of a proud nation /
by Danielle Smith-Llera.
pages cm.—(Fact finders. American Indian life)
Includes bibliographical references and index.
Summary: "Explains Cherokee history and highlights Cherokee life in
modern society"—Provided by publisher.
Audience: Grades 4-6.
ISBN 978-1-4914-4991-2 (library binding)
ISBN 978-1-4914-5003-1 (paperback)
ISBN 978-1-4914-5007-9 (ebook pdf)
1. Cherokee Indians—History—Juvenile literature. 2. Cherokee Indians—
Social life and customs—Juvenile literature. I. Title.
E99.C5S643 2016
975.004'97557—dc23   2015009552

Editorial Credits
Catherine Neitge, editor; Tracy Davies McCabe, designer;
Svetlana Zhurkin, media researcher; Kathy McColley, production specialist

Photo Credits
Alamy: Buddy Mays, 18, Running Whirlwind, 24, 29; AP Photo: Sue
Ogrocki, 20; Dorothy Tidwell Sullivan, Cherokee Master Artist, *She
Speaks for Her Clan*, 17 (top); Getty Images: *National Geographic*/
John Berkey, 9; iStockphoto: JTGrafix, 21; John Guthrie, Guthrie Studios,
13; Lee Guthrie Photography, 4; Library of Congress, 11 (left); National
Geographic Creative: Herbert Tauss, 5, Maggie Steber, 27; Newscom:
Danita Delimont Photography/Angel Wynn, cover (bottom), Danita
Delimont Photography/Luc Novovitch, 15, Zuma Press/Miguel Juarez
Lugo, 19; North Wind Picture Archives: NativeStock, 6, 22, 23, 26 (top), 28;
Shutterstock: American Spirit, 25, Jianzhong Zhu, 11 (right), Silver Spiral
Arts, 26 (bottom); SuperStock: Universal Images Group, cover (top), 1;
Wikimedia: Hosmich, 17 (bottom); XNR Productions, 16

Printed in the United States of America.
012017   010215R

Table of Contents

herokee

Celebration

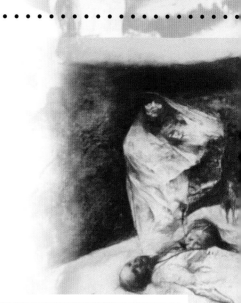

Rhythms of turtle shell rattles and singing in Tsalagi, the Cherokee language, fill the city. People chase balls with sticks and roll stone marbles across fields. Under tents, tables display handwoven baskets and bubbling pots of traditional stews.

Thousands of Cherokee people gather in Tahlequah, Oklahoma, each year to celebrate the Cherokee National Holiday. It commemorates the signing of the 1839 Cherokee Nation constitution. After three days the celebrations end. Yet many Cherokee remember their **traditions** throughout the year. Remembering how their **ancestors** lived helps guide them in their daily lives today.

A young Cherokee boy dances at a powwow in Tahlequah.

tradition: custom, idea, or belief passed down through time

ancestor: family member who lived a long time ago

Cherokee remember the Trail of Tears, which brought their ancestors to Oklahoma.

Chapter 1

Cherokee Early Life

The Cherokee lived in villages throughout the Southeast.

The Cherokee and their ancestors have lived in North America for thousands of years. Their small towns dotted the present-day southeastern states of Alabama, Georgia, North Carolina, South Carolina, and Tennessee when Europeans arrived. They were one of the largest tribes in North America.

Each town worked together—like a family. The women farmed and shared crops of corn, beans, and squash. The men fished and hunted deer, wild turkey, and squirrels. They shared the meat with the tribe. They traded with other tribes nearby for goods they did not have.

Cherokee towns were deeply connected. Each person belonged to one of seven clans—Bird, Paint, Deer, Wolf, Blue, Long Hair, and Wild Potato. People of the same clan considered themselves family members, even if they lived in different towns. Towns would band together during wars with other tribes.

Two male chiefs were elected in each town. A peace chief made decisions during peaceful times. A war chief made decisions during times of war. The chiefs met with advisers and tribal members in a special, seven-sided building. The seven sides represented the seven clans.

The Cherokee believe that people must live peacefully with nature. They also believe in *gadugi*, which means working together for the good of the town.

Cherokee ancestors

Cherokee people have ancestors from other American Indian tribes and Europeans. During war the Cherokee took prisoners. They often adopted the prisoners into their tribe to replace people killed by warfare or disease.

EUROPEANS ARRIVE

The Cherokee people have successfully adapted to many changes. Spanish explorer Hernando de Soto arrived on Cherokee land in 1540. Many other explorers followed, looking for gold and land. They were not always friendly to the native people. The Europeans often killed Cherokee with guns. The Cherokee fought back with bows and arrows.

The Cherokee began to trade with the British in the mid-1600s. The Cherokee gave them deerskins. The British gave them steel pots, knives, cloth, glass beads, and guns. The Cherokee began to cook, dress, and hunt differently.

Contact with the traders brought disaster to the Cherokee. Some of the Europeans carried a deadly disease. Smallpox killed nearly half the Cherokee people in the late 1730s.

The Cherokee fought alongside the British in the French and Indian War, but their **alliance** didn't last. In the late 1750s they fought each other. Cherokee warriors killed many red-coated British soldiers in forest battles. The British destroyed many Cherokee towns and burned their fields. In 1761 the British and the Cherokee made peace.

alliance: agreement between groups to work together

Spanish explorers were the first Europeans to meet the Cherokee.

In the late 1700s, the British desperately needed the Cherokee's help in a new war. American colonists were fighting for freedom from British rule. The Cherokee warriors fought on the British side. They hoped to prevent Americans from taking more of their land. Furious colonists destroyed many Cherokee towns. The British lost the war, and the new United States government now controlled the Cherokee tribe.

Chapter 2

Power and Tragedy

The Cherokee had always talked about their history and beliefs but never wrote them down. Then they borrowed an important idea from Europeans. In the early 1800s, a Cherokee silversmith named Sequoyah invented a system of writing. His **syllabary** was based on syllables in Cherokee words. A written language gave the Cherokee a new power. Many Cherokee learned to read and write their language. Their first newspaper was published in 1828.

The Cherokee wrote a **constitution** for the new Cherokee Nation in 1827. The capital was New Echota, Georgia. Their government had three branches—just like the U.S. government.

syllabary: set of characters that represent the syllables of a language; a syllable consists of a vowel sound or a consonant-vowel combination

constitution: legal document that describes the basic form of the government and the rights of citizens

Sequoyah lived from 1778 to 1848.

Giant sequoias

The Cherokee today are deeply grateful to Sequoyah and his syllabary. Huge trees called giant sequoias are named after him. They grow only in California and have reached heights of more than 300 feet (91 meters).

WASHINGTON AND THE CHEROKEE

President George Washington believed that the Cherokee should live more like white Americans. They had lost much of their hunting land. Washington urged them to farm instead. He sent farming experts to teach the Cherokee people how to use a plow. They taught the Cherokee how to grow cotton and how to weave their own clothing instead of trading for it.

The Cherokee shared land with each other. But Washington's experts taught them to build fences to separate their farms. Some Cherokee became owners of large farms. Some even were slave owners like their white neighbors. It made them appear "civilized" to southern white Americans.

TRAIL OF TEARS

Life for the new Cherokee Nation turned tragic. White Americans wanted the Cherokee's rich farmland. Gold was discovered on tribal lands. At the urging of President Andrew Jackson, Congress passed the Indian Removal Act in 1830. The Cherokee and four other tribes were eventually forced off their lands. They had to sell tribal lands to white Americans.

In 1838 soldiers forced more than 16,000 Cherokee men, women and children to leave their homes and move to unsettled territory in the West. Historians believe that about 4,500 Cherokee died during the 800-mile (1,287-kilometer) journey. It was so painful and deadly that it became known as the Trail of Tears. An equal number are believed to have died within a year of reaching Indian Territory in present-day Oklahoma.

When the Cherokee arrived they built schools, churches, and businesses. In September 1839 they adopted a new constitution. They chose Tahlequah as the capital of the new Cherokee Nation.

A group of about 1,000 Cherokee escaped the 1838 government roundup by hiding in the Appalachian mountains. They eventually set up a tribal government in Cherokee, North Carolina. They became the Eastern Band of Cherokee Indians.

The owl is the messenger of death in John Guthrie's symbolic painting of the deadly Trail of Tears.

The Civil War rocked the Cherokee Nation in the 1860s. The tribe split over support for the North and the South. Most Cherokee supported the South, their former homeland. After the South lost the bloody war, the U.S. government punished the Cherokee by taking away many western lands.

The Cherokee lost more land and rights in 1907 when Indian Territory became the state of Oklahoma. The Cherokee Nation adopted a new constitution in 1976 with the support of the U.S. government.

Chapter 3

Cherokee Life Today

The Cherokee make up the largest tribe in the United States with a population of nearly 820,000. Many live in large cities in the western United States. Others live in farming areas—sometimes in cabins on land passed down through families.

About 40 percent of the Cherokee are citizens of three federally recognized tribes. The Cherokee Nation and United Keetoowah Band of Cherokee Indians are located inside Oklahoma. The Eastern Band of Cherokee Indians—**descendants** of those who escaped the Trail of Tears—are in North Carolina.

Federally recognized tribes have a government-to-government relationship with the United States, according to the Bureau of Indian Affairs. Cherokee citizens are also U.S. citizens.

descendant: person who comes from a particular group of ancestors

The tribes have governments that make laws. They have their own police forces and hospitals.

Cherokee today vote for their leaders. Their principal chief can serve for two four-year terms. Cherokee voters also elect members of a tribal council who make their laws. There is also a judicial branch of government.

A Cherokee dancer and his son speak with a tribal elder in North Carolina.

NATION AND CLAN

The Cherokee have always believed that people should participate in their government. In early times the chief and his advisers gathered in the Council House. Men, women—and even children—joined in discussing solutions to problems in the town.

Cherokee today are loyal to their nation, but also to their clan families. The seven sides of the traditional Council House represented the seven clans. Cherokee today still belong to either the Wolf, Bird, Deer, Wild Potato, Paint, Blue, or Long Hair clans.

Cherokee followed the Trail of Tears to Oklahoma.

Seven women representing the seven Cherokee clans are depicted in Cherokee master artist Dorothy Tidwell Sullivan's painting.

Cherokee children belong to their mother's clan. At ceremonies, clan members sit together. They consider themselves brothers and sisters. Some traditional Cherokee today still avoid marrying anyone from their clan.

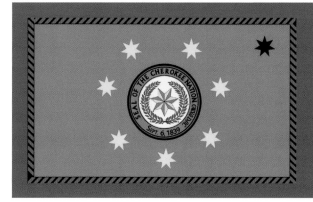

Cherokee Nation flag

Seven stars float against the orange background of the Cherokee Nation flag. They represent the seven clans in the Cherokee tribe. One black star represents the Cherokee lives lost on the Trail of Tears.

POWERFUL LEADERS

Women headed clans for thousands of years. Children today receive a Cherokee name from their **maternal** grandmother. Usually only the family uses this name. Cherokee have an English name for life outside the home.

Cherokee women have been powerful leaders in their families. In the early times, they owned the family homes and gardens. They made decisions for the family.

Women have also been powerful leaders in Cherokee government. In the early times, the eldest woman, the clan mother, chose men who would become leaders for the town. They could serve as advisers to the chief and the council. During war, one woman was selected to decide the fate of prisoners of war.

maternal: relating to the mother

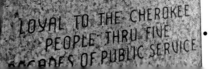

JOHN ROSS
1790 – 1866
PRINCIPAL CHIEF
OF THE
CHEROKEE NATION
1828 – 1866

Wilma Mankiller next to a sculpture of John Ross, longest serving principal chief of the Cherokee

LOYAL TO THE CHEROKEE
PEOPLE THRU FIVE
DECADES OF PUBLIC SERVICE

Wilma Mankiller became the first female principal chief of the Cherokee Nation in 1985. She led the nation in building new health centers and schools. She also helped build centers to teach Cherokee people new skills so they could find better jobs. President Bill Clinton awarded Mankiller the Medal of Freedom, the United States' highest civilian honor, in 1998. She died in 2010 at age 64.

TRIBES WORK TOGETHER

North Carolina and Oklahoma Cherokee celebrated their heritage together at the National Museum of the American Indian in Washington, D.C.

The Cherokee Nation in Oklahoma is far from the Eastern Band of Cherokee in North Carolina. Leaders of the two groups met in 1984—the first time since the Trail of Tears divided the tribe. Since then both groups of Cherokee have worked together to protect their culture and language.

The federal government considers groups of Cherokee living in Alabama, Arkansas, Georgia, and Missouri as unofficial tribal bands. Even though they are not officially Cherokee citizens of the three federally recognized tribes, they feel connected to Cherokee history.

Chapter 4

Protecting the Past

Students at the Cherokee Nation Immersion School in Tahlequah, Oklahoma, study in the Cherokee language.

The Cherokee have always used education to protect their culture. They were one of the first American Indian tribes to have a written language. After their arrival in Indian Territory, the Cherokee built almost 150 elementary schools. More Cherokee could read and write than white Americans in the area. White Americans even paid for their children to attend Cherokee schools.

The system changed in 1907 when Oklahoma became a state. The children now had to attend state public schools. The Cherokee community worried that their children would forget their culture. But today's Oklahoma public schools work to serve Cherokee children. They hire Cherokee teachers, principals, and counselors. The tribes and the federal government pay for school programs just for Cherokee students.

CHEROKEE IMMERSION SCHOOLS

Elders in the Cherokee Nation noticed that the young people only spoke English. They worried that their language would be forgotten.

To make sure that wouldn't happen, the Cherokee opened "immersion" schools where teachers speak only Cherokee to students. The students learn to read and write the syllabary. They learn history from the point of view of the Cherokee.

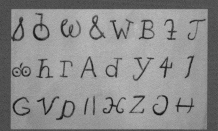

Symbols in the Cherokee syllabary

Older Cherokee are delighted to hear young people speaking to them in their own language.

FOOD

Cherokee have always been thankful for nature's gift of food. In summer some still celebrate corn ripening in the fields. Like their ancestors, they gather in a special, open area to light a fire, dance, and play stickball.

At special times, Cherokee families will remember their history by eating foods their ancestors did. Before tribal events Cherokee cooks grind up hickory nuts to make soup. Outside they gather mushrooms or wild onions to cook with eggs. They shape dough moistened with grape juice into dumplings and bake bean bread.

A traditional Cherokee garden features the "three sisters" of corn, beans, and squash. Each plant helps the others grow.

SPORTS

Cherokee today play traditional sports for fun—and to remember their history. Cherokee men once played stickball to settle arguments instead of going to war. Sometimes players died in the rough games. Players carrying a pair of sticks topped with small baskets battled for a ball. Today Cherokee men, women, and children kick up dust on soccer fields with stickball games. Cherokee play against other American Indian teams in national tournaments.

Like their ancestors, Cherokee today test their aim and strength with archery contests. In "cornstalk shooting" they aim arrows at a stack of cornstalks 80 yards (73 m) away. They pull back the bowstring and see whose arrow pierces the most cornstalks.

A Cherokee dressed in traditional clothing demonstrates stickball.

23

RELIGION

Cherokee continue their tradition of religion and faith. Some attend church where they listen to sermons and sing Christian hymns in the Cherokee language.

Like their ancestors, some Cherokee gather outside in special open areas called stomp grounds. For the Cherokee, the stomp dance is like a group prayer. Participants sit with their clans around a fire. A man circles the flames, singing. A woman shuffles behind him, wearing tortoise-shell rattles around her legs. Others join in until a large group dances rhythmically around the fire.

Cherokee also enjoy gathering with other American Indian tribes at lively events called powwows. Spectators watch dancers dance and stomp their feet in time with drum beats. Members of many tribes dance together. They also compete for prize money.

CLOTHING AS MEMORIAL

At special events the Cherokee wear the traditional clothing of their history. It is called **regalia.** Sometimes it is made of soft leather. Cherokee leather shoes are called moccasins. Women's regalia includes long dresses of printed cotton called tear dresses. Instead of cutting with scissors, the women would tear the cloth into sections before sewing the dress. A design of diamond shapes usually decorates the sleeves, yoke, and skirt of tear dresses. Sometimes seven-sided shapes appear. They represent the seven Cherokee clans. Cherokee sew their tear dresses by hand today just as their ancestors did.

The regalia of Cherokee men includes loose shirts sewn with colorful ribbons. Seven chiefs visited the king of England in 1730. The English asked them to cover their tattooed chests and heads with jackets and turbans. Cherokee men still enjoy wearing this style today.

regalia: special clothes and decorations for ceremonies and celebrations

Moccasins are made of soft leather.

HANDCRAFTS

Cherokee **artisans** today work with their hands to remember their traditions. They maintain old skills passed on by their ancestors.

Girls pair baskets with their traditional tear dresses at a festival.

Before glass or plastic containers, Cherokee used baskets every day for carrying and storing food and belongings. Today the Cherokee enjoy the beauty of baskets. Women might use a woven handbag called the Cherokee purse. Cherokee basket weavers collect vines from wild plants. They boil them in dyes made from plants, berries, bark, and nuts. They often use commercial dyes too as finding plants for natural dyes becomes more difficult.

For thousands of years, the Cherokee have shaped clay into pots by hand. They stamp them with wooden paddles to make designs. Instead of using them for cooking or storing liquids, today's pots usually go on display. Artisans in North Carolina have united into the Cherokee Potters Guild to make pots in the traditional way. They teach classes at museums to inspire others to remember this ancient tradition.

artisan: skilled worker, especially one whose craft requires skill with one's hands

MEDICINE

Some Cherokee today might see a medicine man or woman when they are ill or have problems. Like their ancestors, they believe that nature can heal them. Cherokee healers have taught young people their skills for thousands of years. Recently healers have written down their knowledge in syllabary. Healers today carefully collect plants. Tea made from blackberry roots helps soothe the stomach. They thank nature after taking a plant by leaving a small gift, such as a bead. Healers today have difficulty finding plants for medicine since nature areas are becoming harder to find.

Hundreds of years ago, Cherokee began going to doctors outside their tribe. When white Americans brought deadly diseases, the Cherokee felt their traditional medicine was powerless. Today money from the tribe and the federal government pays for health centers on tribal land. Some Cherokee visit both doctors and traditional healers to stay healthy.

Bark is collected to brew into medicinal tea.

WORK

Today's world hums with busy cities and fast-moving technology. Most Cherokee men and women do not go into the forest or fields to work any more. But the Cherokee tribe still practices the ancient tradition of working together.

Cherokee tribes today own many kinds of businesses that give jobs to thousands of their people. They include Cherokee-owned shops, gas stations, museums, and golf courses. Other businesses hire Cherokee to work with computers or in hospitals or to help build aircraft.

The Cherokee Nation and its businesses do not keep all the money they make. They spend more than half their income on creating more jobs and teaching job skills. They want more Cherokee people to find work.

Long ago Cherokee cared for the gardens of the oldest tribe members. Today some Cherokee businesses pay for senior centers to help older members of the tribe. They also give money to youth centers.

Cherokee today work to move forward together as a tribe. Yet while looking forward, they—and their ancestors—have never forgotten to look back at their history.

TIMELINE

1540: Hernando de Soto is the first European to make contact with the Cherokee.

1629: Trading begins between the Cherokee and British.

1738: Smallpox kills from 25 to 50 percent of the Cherokee population.

1776-1783: Cherokee side with the British during the Revolutionary War.

1796: President George Washington starts "civilization" program.

1821: Sequoyah creates a Cherokee writing system.

1828: Cherokee ratify their first constitution.
John Ross elected principal chief.
Cherokee Phoenix newspaper begins publication.

1830: Indian Removal Act forces American Indians to leave their homelands.

1835: Some Cherokee leaders sign the Treaty of New Echota and agree to move west; treaty did not represent the wishes of most Cherokee.

1838: U.S. government forces the Cherokee to move to Indian Territory; many die on the Trail of Tears and after arrival in the West.

1839: Cherokee write a new constitution.

1985: Wilma Mankiller becomes the first female principal chief of the Cherokee Nation.

2009: President Barack Obama signs a bill that includes text apologizing to American Indians for "many instances of violence, maltreatment, and neglect."

GLOSSARY

alliance (uh-LY-uhns)—agreement between groups to work together

ancestor (AN-sess-tur)—family member who lived a long time ago

artisan (AR-tuh-zuhn)—skilled worker, especially one whose craft requires skill with one's hands

constitution (kahn-stuh-TOO-shuhn)—legal document that describes the basic form of the government and the rights of citizens

descendant (di-SEN-duhnt)—person who comes from a particular group of ancestors

maternal (mat-UR-nuhl)—relating to the mother

regalia (ri-GALE-yuh)—special clothes and decorations for ceremonies and celebrations

syllabary (SIL-uh-berry)—set of characters that represent the syllables of a language; a syllable consists of a vowel sound or a consonant-vowel combination

tradition (truh-DISH-uhn)—custom, idea, or belief passed down through time

READ MORE

Allen, Nancy Kelly. *First Fire: A Cherokee Folktale.*
Mount Pleasant, S.C.: Sylvan Dell Publishing, 2014.

Dwyer, Helen, and D.L. Birchfield. *Cherokee History and Culture.* Native American Peoples.
New York: Gareth Stevens Pub., 2012.

Schwartz, Heather E. *Forced Removal: Causes and Effects of the Trail of Tears.* Cause and Effect: American Indian History.
North Mankato, Minn.: Capstone Press, 2015.

Sonneborn, Liz. *Wilma Mankiller.* Leading Women.
New York: Marshall Cavendish Benchmark, 2011.

INTERNET SITES

FactHound offers a safe, fun way to find Internet sites related to this book. All of the sites on FactHound have been researched by our staff.

Here's all you do:

Visit *www.facthound.com*

Type in this code: 9781491449912

 Check out projects, games and lots more at
www.capstonekids.com

CRITICAL THINKING USING THE COMMON CORE

1. Why do you think learning and maintaining their language is so important to the Cherokee today? (Integration of Knowledge and Ideas)

2. What if the Cherokee had stayed in the East and had not been sent to Indian Territory on the Trail of Tears? How do you think their lives would be different today? (Integration of Knowledge and Ideas)

3. How did the Cherokee protect their lives and culture during difficult times in history? (Key Ideas and Details)

INDEX